WALKS AROUND NIDDERDALE

10 WALKS OF 7 MILES OR UNDER

Dorian Speakman

Dalesman

First published in 2009 by Dalesman
an imprint of
Country Publications Ltd
The Water Mill
Broughton Hall
Skipton
North Yorkshire BD23 3AG

First edition 2009

Text © Dorian Speakman 2009
Maps © Gelder Design & Mapping 2009
Illustrations © Christine Isherwood 2009
Cover: Knaresborough by Colin Raw

ISBN 978-1-85568-260-3

Printed by Amadeus Press

PUBLISHER'S NOTE

The information given in this book has been provided in good faith and is intended only as a general guide. Whilst all reasonable efforts have been made to ensure that details were correct at the time of publication, the author and Country Publications Ltd cannot accept any responsibility for inaccuracies. It is the responsibility of individuals undertaking outdoor activities to approach the activity with caution and, especially if inexperienced, to do so under appropriate supervision. The activity described in this book is strenuous and individuals should ensure that they are suitably fit before embarking upon it. They should carry the appropriate equipment and maps, be properly clothed and have adequate footwear. They should also take note of weather conditions and forecasts, and leave notice of their intended route and estimated time of return.

Contents

Introduction

Dominated by the acidic, coarse Millstone Grit rock, Nidderdale cuts through the windswept uplands to forge a landscape of pasture and woodland and of fields and barns. Along the dale are spectacular rock formations, heather moors, old mines revealing the dale's industrial heritage, ghosts of railways and even forgotten towns, limestone gorges and caves. Nidderdale is quieter than better-known dales such as Wharfedale or Wensleydale, with a more intimate landscape for the walker.

The upper dale is strongly associated with its three reservoirs, and has Pateley Bridge as its hub. Lower down, the woodlands and fields are overlooked by Brimham Rocks. Passing below Harrogate, the river cuts deep into the rock to form the Nidd Gorge where the dale enters the Magnesian limestone belt, a rolling country of low foothills, before finally merging with the plain of the Vale of York.

It is in the Nidd Gorge that the book starts, with the walks progressing up the dale to finish in the high moorlands. All parts of the dale are accessible, whatever the experience of the walker — indeed the last two walks at the top of the dale have both the easiest and the most strenuous walks of the book. These walks offer a taster of fine walking that can be had in the dale, and a chance to experience the great variety within this special landscape.

Nine of the walks are accessible by public transport (even the tenth is possible if an extra five miles are added), though the upper dale has bus services restricted to summer Sundays and monthly in winter — see dalesbus.org for details. The sketch maps show the main route, and where appropriate mention other routes thus ⑥ so that different walks can be combined. Most of the walks are covered by Ordnance Survey Explorer map 26 Nidderdale, but the first requires Explorer 27 Lower Wharfedale or Leeds map 289, and the final walk round Scar House Reservoir is best served by OL30 Yorkshire Dales North & Central. Detailed ten-figure grid references are mentioned in the text to aid navigation where the route may be unclear.

A final note should be made about the terrain: it can be muddy after wet weather, and the temperature and exposure can change rapidly on open hillsides in contrast to the sheltered valleys, so stout footwear and wind and waterproof clothing is essential.

The Nidd Gorge

Distance: 6¹/₂ miles (10.5 km)
Time: 3 hours
Terrain: surfaced tracks and footpaths which can be very muddy;
some short hilly stretches
Start: Convention Centre, Harrogate, grid ref 299 555; buses from
Leeds and Bradford, trains from Leeds, Knaresborough and York
Finish: Knaresborough town centre; frequent buses and trains to
Harrogate, Leeds and York
Parking: several large car parks in Harrogate town centre
Refreshments/facilities: plenty in Harrogate and Knaresborough,
pub in Old Bilton

*This walk begins at the very centre of the famous spa town of Harrogate,
close to the original Kursaal (Cure Hall) and the site of the sulphurous
springs that gave the town its raison d'être. The town still has plenty to offer
the visitor; it is also a useful transport hub for exploring Nidderdale.*

From the Convention Centre (the entrance opposite the Royal Baths), take
Kings Road. Just before the Exhibition Hall, cross by the pelican crossing to
Strawberry Dale Avenue. Turn left onto Franklin Road, a tree-lined avenue
passing several guest houses and hotels. At the junction, go straight ahead to
the left of the house with spire, where the road rapidly narrows and ends.

Take the path on the left which bridges the railway. When it emerges onto a
street, turn right to go as far as Dragon Street car park. Keeping to the right
side of the car park, take the entrance to the Dragon Cycleway. Follow the
path out of the car park, before paralleling the railway. When the cycleway
emerges at a quiet street, take the pavement down to a fenced path ahead.
This path crosses over the railway. After the bridge, turn right to take the
path signed 'Beryl Burton, Knaresborough and Starbeck'. Where the path
forks, take the right fork, ignoring the turn-offs into the estate. Follow this
old railway path for about half a mile.

At a small bridge (GR 31565, 57204) there is a narrow path on the right.
Descend down the side of the bridge to take another path just left of a

stream. Crossing the cycle track at the signposts, take the footpath straight ahead which joins another track and a drive, and follows the stream again.

Cross the road in Old Bilton village, passing the Gardener's Arms pub, to take the track opposite (signposted 'Nidd Gorge'), then follow the arrows onto the path. The path is a lovely green lane with an open section on the edge of a field. Soon after passing under the pylons the path loses height to descend by steps into the Nidd Gorge. At the junction turn right (signed for Knaresborough) descending to riverside.

The Nidd Gorge is nowadays managed by the Woodland Trust. The gorge itself was formed 15,000 years ago as a result of glacial action diverting the course of the River Nidd. Cutting through a series of marl, limestone and sandstone, gritstone and shale and coal, this creates very differing conditions for the soil and the vegetation. The woodlands of the gorge are home to a variety of wildlife and birds.

The path in the Nidd Gorge now follows the course of the river quite closely, and it can be muddy despite the provision of duckboards. In about a mile, the path passes a footbridge, and after the next major bend in the river the path ascends the slope by means of a series of steps.

At the top, passing a path on the right, the route continues on the Ringway path which winds its way along the top of the slope edge. Where it meets a track (GR 32722, 57754) turn left.

The track soon emerges onto Bilton Lane. Turn left where it is signed for Knaresborough Round and Ringway footpath. At the next junction, go straight ahead on the Ringway footpath (signed for walkers and cyclists only, no horses). This narrow tarmac path gradually descends, with fine views of Knaresborough appearing in front of you.

Bird's-eye primrose.

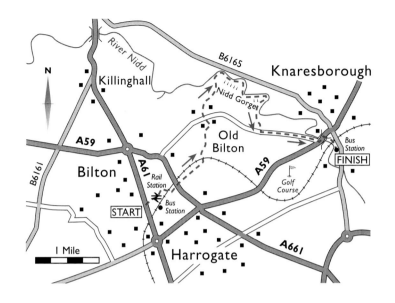

Knaresborough enjoys a spectacular location overlooking the end of the Nidd Gorge, which is crossed by the viaduct of the railway. Very much a visitor destination, Knaresborough's attractions include Mother Shipton's Cave, the castle, the riverside, and the shops and pubs of the town centre.

At the bottom of the slope, take the path straight ahead (cyclists are signed to go right). Where the path splits, take the right fork (not the Coningham Hall Trail) and cross the stream at the bottom. Continue by the riverside to exit by a gate opposite the entrance of Mother Shipton's Cave (buses back to Harrogate can be caught here).

Cross the road here and cross the River Nidd. Turn right down Waterside, then left up the cobbled Water Bag Bank. This steep lane passes the railway station; cross the railway for the town centre. Take Kirkgate and pass the town square for the bus station.

Ripley to Birstwith

Distance: 3 miles (5 km), or 3¹/₂ miles (5¹/₂ km)
Time: 1¹/₂ – 2 hours
Terrain: surfaced tracks and footpaths; can be muddy
Start: Ripley village centre, grid ref 284 605; bus 36 from Harrogate, Leeds and Ripon to Ripley (frequent service, half-hourly on Sundays)
Finish: Birstwith; bus 24 between Pateley Bridge and Harrogate (hourly service, two to three an hour on Sundays); if travelling back to Ripley, catch bus 24 as far as Killinghall and change onto the service 36 (northbound to Ripon, so cross the main A61 at Killinghall) for the three-minute journey to Ripley
Parking: Harrogate town centre (catch the bus to Ripley, return from Birstwith) or at the southern end of Ripley village
Refreshments/facilities: cafés in Ripley, pub in Birtswith

This is a short walk, but a grand introduction to Nidderdale on relatively easy terrain. Ripley, the starting point, has the unusual distinction of being rebuilt in the style of a French village under the direction of Sir William Arncotts Ingilby. Ripley Castle, the home of the Ingilby family for 700 years, stands in beautiful landscaped grounds. Rather more grimly, the nearby All Saints' Church still has bullet marks made by Cromwell's soldiers executing Royalist prisoners after the battle of Marston Moor.

From the stone cross, take the road signed for the castle and gardens. Continue past the castle entrance through a gate along Hollybank Lane (a former Roman road which ran from Ilkley to Aldborough). The lane takes a winding route along the castle boundary. At Sadler Carr continue in the same direction, ignoring the turn-offs. The track bends right and is bounded by a mixture of conifers, coppiced trees and an old hedgerow before it enters deciduous woodland. The lane descends and joins a tarmac lane by a house.

(For the slightly longer route, best done in dry weather, take the bridleway on the left signed 'The Horseshoe' and follow this narrow route, which usually has a muddy section near its end at Clint. At the road, turn left down

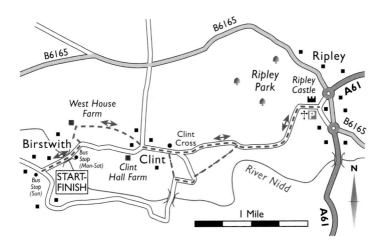

the hill. Follow the road until the sharp left-hand bend. Take a path on the right. The path follows the field boundary by a house and climbs quite steeply back up the hill to the hamlet of Clint.)

Otherwise, continue along Hollybank Lane as it gains height and enters the hamlet of Clint, joining another road and a junction of paths. Instead of taking the paths, continue along the little-used Clint Bank Lane, past the increasingly large houses of Clint as far as the T-junction.

Halfway on the right side of the road, you pass the ancient Clint Stone cross, accompanied by a small plaque.

Take the footpath signed at the gate opposite. Cross the field, passing just to the right of a ruin. A gate soon comes into view. Go through the gate. Follow the wall and fence along the stream.

Along the hillside, fine views of Nidderdale appear ahead.

Cross the stream by the stiles. Go straight ahead over the next field. Take the kissing-gate to descend by the hedge to a gate. Following the direction of the arrow, continue in the same direction to go through two gates to the farm. Turn left onto the tarmac lane to descend. Take the next left to emerge at Station Road. Turn right to descend into Birstwith, where there is a bus stop soon after the Old Station Inn pub, and a return to your starting point at either Harrogate or Ripley.

Fountains Abbey

Distance: 4 miles (6.5 km)
Time: 2 hours
Terrain: paths and tracks
Start: Ripon, grid ref 312 712; bus 36 from Harrogate and Leeds
Finish: Fountains Abbey; Ripon Roweller shuttle bus 139 connects
Ripon with Fountains Abbey; additional Dalesbus summer service
from Leeds (half-price admission to abbey with bus ticket)
Parking: Ripon city centre or Fountains Abbey
Refreshments/facilities: plenty in Ripon, cafés at Fountains Abbey
visitor centre and Studley Lake entrance

*Though not in Nidderdale, this walk is in an area very much associated with
the Nidderdale Area of Outstanding Natural Beauty. The small city of Ripon
owes its status to its magnificent cathedral, founded over 1,300 years ago.*

From the marketplace, head down Duck Hill. At the bottom, turn right and
then left down a pedestrian walkway between housing. Bend right to follow
the street to the river. At the junction, turn right. Take the path leading off
right by the riverside, signposted 'Fountains Abbey and Studley Royal'.
This riverside path leads under a bridge and past a playground. Turn right
down the lane, which narrows to a path after passing a farm. Past the
footbridge, ignore the path to the left but carry on ahead up the concrete
steps, to follow the path through woodland, keeping close to the river where
the path splits in the first clearing.

At the second clearing, take the broad path which leads away from the river
in a direction approximately at 11 o'clock (GR 30045, 70312), across the
clearing into the next patch of woodland (GR 30016 70182). This wide path
ends by the start of a lane at Hell Wath, marked by a visitor information
board. From there follow the lane past Hell Wath Cottage up to the road.
Continue straight ahead, reaching a housing estate before meeting
Whitcliffe Lane which emerges on the right.

*Like the Nidd Gorge, this is Magnesian Limestone country, a white rock
which when exposed reveals white cliffs, which Whitcliffe is named after.*

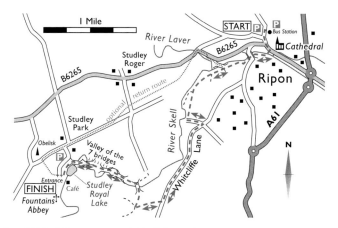

Follow Whitcliffe Lane past Whitcliffe Hall Farm. Take the next path right signed 'Ripon Rowel'. This wide grassy path leads up a slope to a gate by Mackershaw Woods. Go through the gate and down into the shallow valley. At the junction, turn right into the valley bottom. Take the footbridge on the left to cross the river and turn left onto the track. Continue along the track to the tall kissing-gate. This leads to the Valley of the Seven Bridges, as the path follows the twisting route of the River Skell.

Studley Royal Estate has many deer roaming around and it is here, or near St Mary's Church, that you may catch sight of them.

Follow the path up the valley and over the bridges to Studley Lake. The path then leads around the lake to Fountains Abbey and the Studley Lake car park.

Fountains Abbey, a World Heritage Site, is a twelfth-century Benedictine abbey set in beautifully landscaped water gardens dating from the eighteenth century. Now the largest monastic ruins in the country, the site has many fine walks as well as the only twelfth-century watermill in Britain.

(A return walk to Ripon of 3^1/$_2$ miles (5.5 km) is via the hamlet of Studley Roger. Leaving the car park, take the path up to St Mary's Church. Follow the road down through the deer park, peeling off left onto a grassy path 100 yards before the archway. The path leads through Studley Roger, then emerges on the B6265 at the edge of Ripon. Turn right and follow the road as far as the bridge. Turn right. Take the path on the right side to follow the River Laver down to its confluence, and retrace your steps from the footbridge along the River Skell back to Ripon's centre.)

11

Brimham Rocks

Distance: 4 miles (6.5 km)
Time: 3 hours
Terrain: surfaced tracks and footpaths, which can be very muddy
Start: Brimham Rocks, grid ref 208 645
Parking: National Trust car park at Brimham Rocks
Public transport: bus 26 Harrogate–Pateley Bridge calls at
Brimham Rocks (summer Sundays, monthly in winter)
Daily service (less frequent on Sundays)
Alternative start*: Ye Olde Oak Inn, Low Laithe, a mile north of
Summerbridge; bus 24 Harrogate–Pateley Bridge calls hourly at
Low Laithe; the inn is about fifty yards north of the bus stop
Refreshments/facilities: kiosk at Brimham Rocks, Ye Olde Oak
Inn, Low Laithe

This walk starts and ends at the truly spectacular Brimham Rocks, large tor-like pillars of rock standing on the hillside above Nidderdale. Formed by the action of water, ice and wind, these gritstone rocks have been carved into unusual shapes, inspiring the Victorians to give them evocative names such as the Dancing Bear.

Take the path next to the noticeboard and ticket machine which leads away from the main access track. Maintaining height, follow this wooden-edged path heading for the visitor centre on the hilltop ahead.

At Brimham Rocks visitor centre there is an exhibition centre as well as toilets and a shop. There is also a viewpoint with a sweeping panorama across Nidderdale, the Washburn Valley and the Vale of York to the east.

Facing the visitor centre, turn left. Before the track bends off right, turn left to descend along a gravel path. Turn right in between two large rock pillars. Descend via the clearing straight ahead, ignoring paths to the right and left (GR 20600, 64873). After about seventy yards, join the track and turn right.

Follow the track to the right of the farm where it splits, then continue on the level. After passing a barn, enclosed by stone walls, the lane begins to

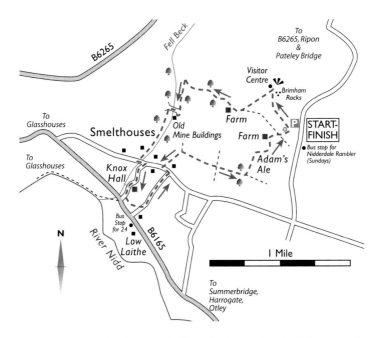

descend steadily. After just over half a mile the track ends. Take the path leading off left before the house. Go through the wooden gate and down the enclosed path to the woods. Turn left on entering the woods.

The path winds through the woods, gradually losing height; note the left turn where it meets a wider path, the way indicated by arrows. By the old ruins, follow the waymarks right as the path drops down to the beck. Cross over on the footbridge. Follow the path downstream. Emerge at a road in Smelthouses.

As its name indicates, the hamlet of Smelthouses was once the site of industrial activity dating back to medieval times, when the monks of Fountains Abbey had their lead smelthouses here. Now it is a haven of tranquillity in beautiful semi-natural woodland.

Turn left to cross the beck once again, then take the next right. Follow the track down past the houses to enter a small wood. Where the track emerges from the wood, take the left fork up past Knox Hall. Once past the house, take the path to the right of the garages which follows the edge of the wood. Where the path meets the track, turn left to take the track uphill.

13

Brimham Rocks.

For those joining the walk at Low Laithe, follow the directions from here, reached by taking the signposted track up from Ye Olde Oak Inn.

The track levels out. At the road, turn left to drop down by some houses. Take the track right, signed 'Brimham'. This concrete lane passes scattered houses. At the next junction of paths turn right, taking the route signed 'Bridleway to Brimham'. This grassy (and often muddy) enclosed lane soon leads uphill on a gentle gradient.

After just over half a mile, take the footpath signposted on the left. Cross a field to enter a small wood, where the Adam's Ale springs appear near the path. Just before the edge of the wood, the path swings up then leaves the wood to pass through a farm.

Fine views over Nidderdale appear with the ridge of Greenhow Hill ahead.

By the farmhouse, turn right onto the track to continue up. At the junction take the narrow path just across (slightly to the right). The path continues up the slope in the same direction past the rocks and meets a well-defined path. Turn right, passing the National Trust boundary sign, to continue up to the car park.

Pateley Bridge

Distance: 5¼ miles (8.5 km)
Time: 3 hours
Terrain: paths and tracks; can be muddy, particularly in Guisecliff Wood; one ascent of around 650 feet (200 m)
Start: Pateley Bridge, grid ref 157 655
Parking: car park in Pateley Bridge town centre
Public transport: bus 24 from Harrogate (hourly Monday to Saturday, 2-3 hourly on Sundays), Dalesbus direct from Leeds on summer Sundays
Refreshments/facilities: cafés in Pateley Bridge and Glasshouses; toilets in Pateley Bridge

This walk encapsulates everything about Nidderdale: riverside, woods, crags, open moorland with fine panoramic views, and green fields.

Note that some of the route (Guisecliff Wood and the approach to Strikes Wood) does not coincide with the paths marked on the Ordnance Survey map.

From the bridge in Pateley Bridge, take the path on the left side, marked by a gap in the wall. Follow the riverbank downstream out of Pateley. Passing the site of the old station, the riverside path runs along the riverbank parallel to the course of the former Nidderdale Railway.

The railway opened in 1862 and used to run from Harrogate to serve upper Nidderdale. The line, which extended up to Scar House with the reservoir construction works, lasted over a century until the last goods train to Pateley Bridge left in 1964.

At a bend in the river, turn right towards the bridge, ignoring the stile on the left. Continue along the track past the lake to Glasshouses. At the end of the track, turn right to cross the River Nidd on a road bridge. Passing the path on the left, take the next left fork of the road, and then the next right. Follow this track up the hill, passing Hollin House Farm. Continue to the stile on the right of the last house, and up an enclosed path to the woods ahead.

15

Once over the next stile, turn immediately right. The path climbs through the holly trees, where it can be muddy in places. Where the path meets another, turn left to continue upwards (GR 16863, 63687).

After about fifty yards, turn right. Shortly after there is a branch off right towards Guisecliff Tarn. If going up to the tarn, follow this up to the tarn edge, and rejoin the previous path heading up the slope from the same side of the water. Otherwise continue along the path up the slope. Levelling out by birch trees, the path then descends into an area of mossy boulders under the trees. Next, the path continues on the level. At the edge of the wood the path forks. Take the right fork which starts to climb once again.

A fine view of lower Nidderdale now appears with wide views towards the south and east.

Ascending through the bracken, the path approaches a stone wall. Bending right by the first birch tree (GR 17217, 63179), turn right again, taking the path that heads up toward the rocky outcrop and keeping to the right of the radio mast.

As you reach the ridge a fine view of the upper dale now appears, with Gouthwaite Reservoir on the valley floor and the brown moors leading up to the hill crest of Little Whernside at the head of the dale.

Approaching the next stone wall, keep to the right of it before joining the path, to continue along the ridge. At this point the route follows the top of Guise Cliff. The right side is flanked by the cliff edge and rock crevasses; on the left is heather-clad moor, the path running through an area where the trees are trying to regain a foothold on the edge of the bare moor.

At the walk's summit, the 1,000 foot (305 m) contour is breached, the views rewarding the effort made in the ascent.

The path runs along the ridge before edging more towards the moor and to the left of the woodland. On the descent the path goes via a stile to pass in front of Yorke's Folly.

Yorke's Folly was built by the local squire in the early nineteenth century as a means of providing some local employment during a severe economic downturn. Originally three towers, part of it was destroyed by a gale.

Past the folly, the path descends the moorland to a road. Cross the road to the gate, and take the path signposted for Bewerley. The path descends the open ground towards Strikes Wood. Past a gate, the path drops more steeply

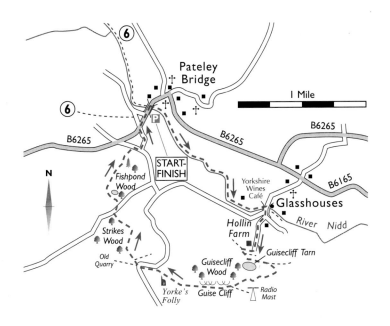

before entering the wood, then descends steeply down an ancient cobbled track. At the edge of the wood, ignore the stile. Instead, bend left to follow the wall, descending again into the wood. The sound of waterfalls can be heard as the descent continues. At the bottom, cross over the footbridge to meet the road.

Turn right, crossing the bridge. Go along the lane up to a small gate on the left, past the farm. Once again in woodland, the path leads through rhododendrons and over a track to a gate marked by a footpath signpost. Following the way to Fishpond Wood, a gravel path leads to and passes to the left of the pond up to a gate at the far side of the wood. Turn right to take a series of stone steps up the short slope, then follow the waymarks down the hill towards the barn below.

When the path meets the tarmac lane, turn right. Follow the lane down to the junction. Turn left to head down towards Grassington Road on the edge of Pateley Bridge. Turn right to cross the River Nidd for the centre of Pateley Bridge.

Ashfold Valley

Distance: 6¹/₂ miles (10.5 km)
Time: 3¹/₂ hours
Terrain: mostly surfaced tracks and field paths; two moderate
ascents totalling 720 feet (220 m), though the descents are steeper
Start: Pateley Bridge, grid ref 157 655
Parking: car park, Pateley Bridge town centre
Public transport: bus 24 from Harrogate (hourly Monday to
Saturday, 2-3 hourly on Sundays), Dalesbus direct from Leeds
on summer Sundays
Refreshments/facilities: cafés and toilets in Pateley Bridge

Pateley Bridge itself is worthy of spending some time exploring. Situated on the hillside overlooking the dale with plenty of shops and services on offer, it is very much the capital of upper Nidderdale. The Nidderdale Museum, in the upper part of the village, is worth a visit and showcases the history of the dale in terms of ordinary life, its industry and transport. In fact, like much larger cities, Pateley Bridge at one time had two railway stations. Above the town are quarries once served by a narrow-gauge railway; the stone was held in such high favour that it was used for Victoria Station and the National Gallery in London.

Cross the bridge at Pateley Bridge. Pass the playground to take the footpath signed behind the garage. The path shortly meets a back street. Turn right and take the next left which is signposted on the left to Ladies Riggs. The way up soon becomes a path. Past a barn conversion, an enclosed path leads up the hill. Follow the wall where it enters a field. Keep to the left of the field as it ascends to a wood. Go over a stile to join a surfaced lane. Turn right.

Golden plover.

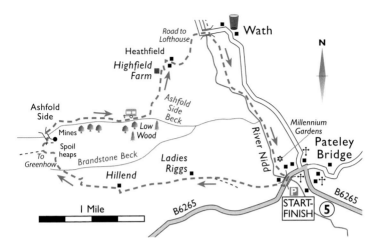

The lane continues the steady ascent, with a side-valley appearing to the left before it enters a bigger valley. The lane levels and descends by a farm, passing over a cattle grid. Where the track splits, take the right fork signed for Ashfold Side and Cockhill. At Hollin Hall House the track crosses a stream and bends left. Close to the summit, pass the turn-off to Cockhill. The track soon begins to descend. By a tree, take the grassy path which snakes between the tree and a stone ruin.

The lead veins were mined here at Ashfold side from Roman times. Now all that remains are gravel spoil tips and ruins of mine buildings overlooking the fast flowing stream. In contrast to the uplands above, Ashfold Valley is wooded and retains a peaceful atmosphere.

The path circles round the old mine workings by a stone wall and gate, then descends by the broken stone wall, winding down through the gravel (care needed) towards the bridge.

Cross the bridge to follow the path up the other bank. Join a track. Continue along the track down the hill. The track passes through a caravan park. At Low Wood (just past twin bridges which cross the beck) take the indistinct grassy path left (GR 13452, 66435).

The path ascends to a stile. After the stile, pass a spring. Turn right to go to a gate (GR 13606, 66514). Past the gate, turn sharp left to follow the wall up the hill. Go through the gate at the top, then bend right to the gate on the right side of the field. Turn left to climb up the slope.

19

The four-spotted chaser dragonfly can be see from May to late August.

Once again follow the drystone wall heading up to Highfield Farm, passing two barns. At the farmyard, turn right and take the track on the right leading out, winding downhill to the hamlet of Heathfield.

At the crossroads, turn right and descend along the road to Spring Hill Farm. Take the well-signed footpath on the left, leading through gates. Turn sharp left to a stile and footpath signpost. The path then descends steeply via a tree in the middle of the field to the next stile, crossing by some rushes and a wooden pylon to a gate.

A view of Gouthwaite Reservoir now appears on the left, with the steep tree-lined sides of Nidderdale rising above. Ahead lies the hamlet of Wath. Wath does have a pub (requesting that walkers remove muddy boots) and a bus stop on the main road — though if enticed to stay on in Wath, please note that the bus service back down the dale to Pateley Bridge is restricted to summer Sundays or monthly Sundays in winter.

Go through the gate and pass to the right of the barn. Descend down to the road. Cross the road. Take the Wath road over the packhorse bridge opposite, and then take the Nidderdale Way on the right. The path leads from the riverside over to a slightly raised wide grassy track which leads down the dale. After about three-quarters of a mile (1 km), the path splits. Take the right path, which follows the riverbank.

The path continues towards Pateley Bridge. At the footbridge there is a junction of paths. Continue straight ahead along the riverbank. The path bends past Millennium Green before approaching a row of houses. Take the narrow path to the right of the houses. This threads its way through between the houses to the bridge in the centre of Pateley Bridge.

Lofthouse & Ramsgill

Distance: 5 miles (8 km)
Time: 3 hours
Terrain: paths and tracks; two short climbs totalling 400 feet (120 m)
Start: Lofthouse, grid ref 101 734
Parking: Lofthouse, off Masham Road
Public transport: Nidderdale Rambler bus from Pateley Bridge
(summer Sundays, monthly in winter)
Refreshments/facilities: Crown pub, Lofthouse; toilets in Lofthouse
Finish: Lofthouse (or How Stean, about 600 yards shorter).

This circular route makes use of the Nidderdale Way for much of its length, taking in the lower reaches of both sides of the valley below Lofthouse.

In Lofthouse, as well as a pub, there is also another diversion for visitors – ice-cream made on a farm, well worth a detour up the Masham road. Lofthouse's industrial heritage can be traced back to monastic times when Fountains Abbey monks obtained the land in 1251, and there is evidence of ironstone mining and smelting in the Blayshaw Gill area. By the nineteenth century when lead and coal mines operated nearby, Lotfhouse was far busier, with three shoemakers and a blacksmith. Once construction of Scar House Reservoir was complete, the Nidderdale Light Railway ceased passenger operations in 1929. Lofthouse is the last village in the dale on the road out to Colsterdale and Masham, which was only upgraded for motor traffic in the 1950s.

In front of Lofthouse Memorial Institute, take the trackway. Just before the gate, go through the narrow gap-stile on the right. Follow the wall for about seventy yards before taking a stile on the left. Continue in the same direction as before, following the wall. Through a stile, go straight ahead to a wooden kissing-gate where the path leads onto the road.

Continue along the road for about a hundred yards. Take the footpath signed 'Nidderdale Way' on the right. Joining the track, the way passes to the right of the trees and a miniature-sized old quarry. Go straight ahead to a stile marked by a post. The path then crosses the corner of the next field by an

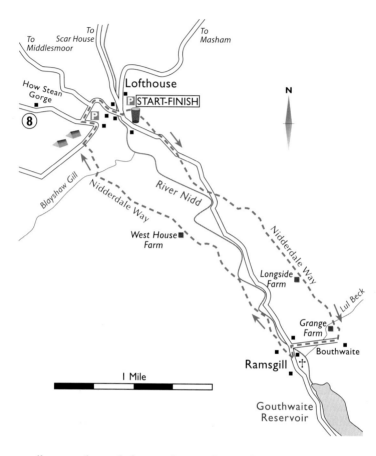

ex-railway goods van, before curving round on a raised level, following the trackbed of the old Nidderdale Light Railway.

Cross the road again. The path crosses a field and then over a stile just to the left of a gate. The path leads left up the slope to a waymarked gate. Here it levels out and runs below a coniferous woodland.

From here, Gouthwaite Reservoir comes into view. The reservoir was the earliest of the Nidderdale reservoirs, built in 1901. It attracts many species of wildfowl, particularly for over-wintering, and so has become a visitor attraction in its own right.

Pass a house and join a track. The route continues ahead, behind the next farm via a gate. Continue to a large stile. The path follows a line of trees along the field edge, then descends into an enclosed lane. At the gate, bend right to cross the beck by the bridge.

On the left is the beautiful wooded valley of Lul Beck. Passing the farmhouses, the first dates from 1613.

Take the track to pass between the farm buildings into the hamlet of Bouthwaite. Emerge at a junction with a tarmac lane. Go straight ahead to cross the main valley of Nidderdale, following the lane for 400 yards.

Along the lane the former trackbed of the Nidderdale Light Railway and Ramsgill's old station are passed. Like Wath Station, this was suddenly closed in the early 1920s whilst the line was serving the construction of Scar House Reservoir.

At the junction, go over the road bridge left into Ramsgill. Just before the next bridge, turn sharp right back to take the Nidderdale Way, signposted to the left of the house now in front of you.

After about 800 yards the track bends left uphill towards a farm. Instead, take the bridleway signed by an arrow straight ahead along the field edge. Go through the gate and down the well-defined track. The track ascends again to another farm, and then leads off right over two stiles. Crossing a track which descends the slope, the path is waymarked by a post ahead, and then joins a track leading out of the farm. The track ascends gradually before levelling out past a barn, the surface becoming more of a grassy path.

At this point a fine panorama of the upper reaches of Nidderdale appears, with the hillside village of Middlesmoor marked by its prominent church ahead. Below on the right is Lofthouse, and behind the village the upper part of Nidderdale winds its way between the slopes behind.

The grassy path now descends by a tree to a track ahead. At the junction, go straight ahead along the track towards the tree-lined valley. After crossing a bridge, the enclosed track winds up to a junction. Turn right to drop down towards a caravan park. Turn left at the next junction. Where the lane emerges onto the road, turn right to go over the bridge to pass How Stean car park (an additional bus stop for the Nidderdale Rambler bus service from Pateley Bridge on summer Sundays and monthly in winter).

Continue along the lane for Lofthouse, turning right at the junction to return to the village.

How Stean

> **Distance: 5 miles (8 km)**
> **Time: 3 hours**
> **Terrain: footpaths and tracks, one major climb of 560 feet (170 m)**
> **Start: How Stean car park, signed from the Middlesmoor road,**
> **grid ref 097 733**
> **Parking: How Stean car park**
> **Refreshments/facilities: How Stean Gorge café**
> **Public transport: Nidderdale Rambler bus from Pateley Bridge**
> **(summer Sundays, monthly in winter season)**

This walk is along How Stean Beck, a tributary valley of the upper Nidd. How Stean Gorge lies at the foot of the approach road to Middlesmoor, a short distance from the village of Lofthouse. Surrounded by broad open expanses of moorland, the wide sweep of the landscape is in contrast to the narrow cleft dug by How Stean Beck into the underlying limestone to form How Stean Gorge.

From the car park, follow the road over the bridge and up the valley, past the How Stean Gorge visitor entrance.

Open to visitors (admission fee payable), How Stean Gorge can be explored in detail in its most dramatic section. In the gorge is Tom Taylor's Cave, made famous after the discovery of some Roman coins in 1868. A café is also available to visitors, and gives an option for walkers returning on this walk to go along the other side of the valley.

As the road levels out before the hamlet of Stean, take the footpath on the right, signposted for Middlesmoor (along the route of the Nidderdale Way).

Descend down to the beck. Cross the footbridge, then at the top of the steps turn left to leave the Nidderdale Way. Go over the tall stile. The path then descends towards a gate. The path is just to the right of the gate, leading into the woodland and down to the side of the beck.

Along here the beck runs along the limestone flags. The path meanders by and then ascends through coppiced trees. Cross a stile and a tiny stream

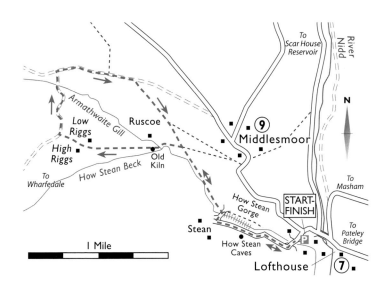

before descending down again to meet a wooden fence. Follow this round to a stone bridge. Cross this, passing an old limekiln. The path bends round to the right to start climbing. Go through the waymarked gate, then head up the slope towards the farm buildings ahead — Low Riggs. As you approach the farm, head for the gate just to the left of the farmhouse in front of the garden. Follow the waymarks through the farmyard and take the track ahead to go up the hill, passing a barn.

Past High Riggs, continue along the track going up the hill. At the junction, turn right. Follow this track as it dips down to a cattle grid before climbing up again. After the second cattle grid, take the right turn at the next junction.

Here fine views open out across the high moors and down the main valley of Nidderdale.

The ring ouzel is also known as the 'mountain blackbird'.

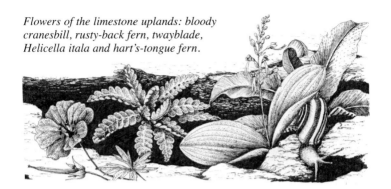

Flowers of the limestone uplands: bloody cranesbill, rusty-back fern, twayblade, Helicella itala and hart's-tongue fern.

From here, after the third cattle grid (GR 08014, 75054) which has a waymark arrow, turn right to go down to a gate with a county council sign giving directions onwards past the farm. Past the farmhouse, follow the arrow to descend to the gate to the left of a ruined barn (Ruscoe).

After the gate, bear right. Take the second gate to descend across the field, heading for the barn ahead. Descend to the open woodland, continuing in the same direction. Go along the right side of the stone wall, where a small stream is crossed. Follow the wall. The path drops down to a stile which joins the outward route shortly after. Cross the next stile ahead (ignore the stile left) and follow the route down to the river.

The path can be followed back along How Stean Beck before the clearing, going up a slope back to the tall stile (ignore the gate). At the footbridge, you can cross this again to retrace the route back down the valley along the Stean road.

Otherwise, if you are intent on visiting How Stean Gorge or café, you can take the path left (signed 'Nidderdale Way') up to the gate. Where it is signposted up the hill, leave the Nidderdale Way to cross the field and go through the gate marked with an orange arrow. Go straight ahead to the next gate and head for the barn. Going to the right side of the barn, bend right to go through a gate and descend down to How Stean Gorge café and the gorge entrance. To return to the car park, leave by the drive to rejoin the Stean road, and follow the road down the valley.

Middlesmoor

Distance: 7 miles (11.5 km)
Time: 4 hours
Terrain: surfaced tracks and riverside footpaths; hilly, with some steep sections, 720 feet (220 m) of total ascent; on some sections the path is not well defined so use of a map is essential
Start: Middlesmoor, car park above village, grid ref 091 743
Refreshments/facilities: Crown pub, Middlesmoor; toilets at Middlesmoor and Scar House car park.
Public transport: Nidderdale Rambler bus from Pateley Bridge to Middlesmoor (summer Sundays, otherwise monthly)

Though this walk is the longest in the book, no walk in upper Nidderdale would be complete without passing through the majestic bend in the valley above Lofthouse. The bleakness of the moorland tops is countered by the patchwork of woodland and fields on the slopes down to the river.

Middlesmoor lies perched on a hillside overlooking the upper dale. With the only access road having a punishing 1:4 (25%) gradient, traffic is light. Many of the buildings in the village are now dwellings which were once workshops, hinting of busier times in the past. Now the focus of the village is the pub, as well as the church which houses several important relics including a cross dating from the tenth or eleventh century.

Go up the village road out of Middlesmoor. Take the little gate on the right (GR 09210, 74277), or on the left if coming down from the car park. The footpath follows a drystone wall to a plantation. Cross the stream at the bridge, and over the field to the gate past Smithfield Farm. Continue on the same level to join the track. Turn right onto the track and follow it until it passes through a gate next to a plantation (GR 09562 75578), with a sign on the right marked 'Footpath'. Descend towards the trees and cross the stream. After about thirty yards, take the stile on the right (an arrow points to it on a tree). Cross the field, and through the stile near the corner of the next field. Continue towards Scar House Road. Cross it to take the path down to the farm.

Turn left to take the track by the river, ignoring the turn-off to the road. Cross the stream and follow the River Nidd along the riverbank, past the cave entrance on the other bank.

Goyden Pot and Manchester Hole are popular with cavers. It is here that the underlying limestone is exposed, and the River Nidd, in true limestone country style, disappears underground for a short section.

A gate ahead (GR 09918 76709) leads through to a more wooded section and a narrowing of the valley floor. In the next field, the path leads up to a bridge which crosses over the River Nidd. Continue following the river upstream, keeping to the riverbank as you approach the next farmhouse (the OS map indicates the path stays to the right — ignore this). Once past New Houses, the path follows a track (straight ahead by the river bridge) continuing along the riverside. Where the track forks, take the footpath ahead through

Field gentian has bluish flowers which bloom on grassland from July to October

the stile. Follow the river before climbing up a short slope to a footbridge over a stream. Descend back down to the riverside again. Head to the right of the next farmhouse, Low Woodale, ahead. Go through the gates and at the junction take the track straight ahead through the gate.

The track takes a winding route up the valley. Cross Woo Gill and pass Middle Woodale, following the drystone wall up the slope. Where the wall bends off left, follow the line of the broken wall up to the gate straight up the slope. From the gate continue up the hill, bearing slightly right to take an indistinct path along a slight depression in the slope to meet a track (GR 07638 77665). Turn left and follow it towards Scar House Reservoir. By the reservoir, turn left to descend by Scar House to cross the dam wall. Turn

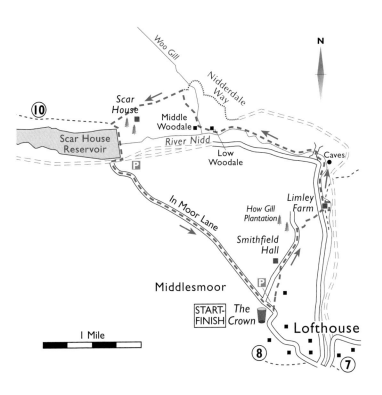

right. After about 200 yards turn left onto the track, In Moor Lane, leading up the slope towards Middlesmoor.

In Moor Lane is a spectacular route across Rain Stang Hill which takes a direct route back to Middlesmoor. Views open up to the north and west towards Great Whernside and the moors up to the Wharfedale watershed. Once the summit is crested at 1,425 feet (434 m), there are equally impressive views down Nidderdale.

The track climbs steeply at first, but levels out and has a long gradual descent towards Middlesmoor, emerging at the top of the village and the car park. The bus back to Pateley Bridge can be caught from the middle of the village.

Scar House & Angram

Distance: 4 miles (6.5 km)
Time: 2 hours
Terrain: easy, mostly level walking on tracks or traffic-free road
Start: Scar House Reservoir car park, grid ref 070 766
Refreshments/facilities: none (nearest is Middlesmoor or
Lofthouse); toilets at Scar House car park
Public transport: none; Scar House can only be reached by public
transport by walking from Middlesmoor via In Moor Lane
(see walk 9), adding an extra 5 miles (8 km) to the route;
Middlesmoor is served by the Nidderdale Rambler bus
from Pateley Bridge

As a result of the easiness of this last route, the spectacular wild scenery at the head of Nidderdale is made that more accessible. If the previous walk was the hardest, this walk is probably the easiest in this book, with no steep gradients and a well-defined route. The only challenge might be the wind, which can blow unimpeded straight down from the slopes of Great Whernside. Being at a relatively high altitude, temperatures around here can be markedly colder than lower down the dale.

From the car park, descend down to the dam wall and cross the dam. Turn left onto the track, signed past the shelter. At the junction, turn left on the track signed 'Angram Dam Scar House circular'. Follow the track which parallels the shore of Scar House Reservoir. By a group of trees the track passes several piles of stones, the ruins of Lodge.

The goosander looks white from a distance but a closer view will reveal that it has a pinkish tinge to its plumage.

The former hamlet of Lodge was at the junction of old drove roads and had a boarding house. Its owner, Margaret Thompson, was reputed to be responsible for the murders of three Scottish pedlars whose bodies were found decapitated on Dead Man's Hill in 1728. A glance at the map shows that Lodge is by a junction of those old routes, now footpaths, from Coverdale and Wharfedale.

Shortly after passing Lodge, there is a junction of tracks. Turn left. At the next junction, by sheep pens, turn right, taking the footpath signed 'Angram'.

There are fine views across Scar House Reservoir to Angram Reservoir and Great Whernside. Angram lies at the very head of Nidderdale, and the upper slopes of Great Whernside are the birthplace of the infant River Nidd. The summits of Great and Little Whernside, reaching over 2,300 feet (700 m) and 2,000 feet (600 m) in altitude respectively, provide Nidderdale with some mountain-type terrain typical of the high Pennines

The grassy track leads up to a stile by the crossing of Wench Gill before approaching the dam wall of Angram. Turn left to cross the dam wall. On the other side, turn left onto the tarmac lane.

Note the cast-iron plate on a pillar by the far end of the dam commemorating the building of Angram Reservoir in 1918. The turret was completed in 1912.

The pink flowers of ragged robin are found on damp grassland from May to August.

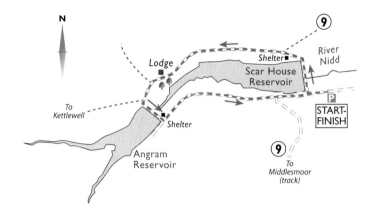

The road takes a steady gentle incline down towards Scar House Reservoir car park, for about 1$^1/_2$ miles (2 km).

Scar House and Angram reservoirs were constructed in the early 1900s to ensure the supply of clean water for the city of Bradford. Scar House was the terminus of the Nidderdale Light Railway, built to supply raw materials to the reservoir construction sites. It was also a busy settlement of over one thousand people during the construction of the dams. During its peak there was a church, theatre, cinema, canteen, laundry and bakery, gymnasium, reading room and tennis court as well as housing for the construction workers, all provided for by Bradford Corporation. Nowadays little trace remains, apart from the foundations of the workers' hostels near the approach road to the dam. Information boards at Scar House car park give further details of the history of the dam construction.